BOLD KIDS

Organism Competition

DISCOVER INTRIGUING FACTS
CHILDREN'S EARTH SCIENCES BOOK

When we hear the word "competition," we usually picture a sport or a contest, and a prize would be a nice perk, such as bragging rights. Organisms, on the other hand, compete with each other for resources, such as food, water, light, and space.

Competition can be direct or indirect, among organisms of the same species or across the globe. If you're interested in the basics of Organism Competition, this book is for you.

ORGANISMS COMPETE WITH EACH OTHER FOR RESOURCES

Competition among organisms is a natural phenomenon that occurs whenever two or more individuals require the same limited resource. All organisms need certain resources for growth, reproduction, and survival, including food, water, and light.

In contrast, intraspecific competition between organisms of the same species is often more intense than interspecific competition. When a species' population grows, competition among individuals reduces the number of available resources for the next individual.

Competition among organisms occurs in two ways: direct and indirect. In direct competition, organisms directly compete with one another for the same resource. In the case of predator–prey competition, one group takes more of a resource than the other, and the other takes it.

A growing wolf population may eat the entire food supply of other carnivores. In apparent competition, a reduction in one species' population affects the abundance of another. In the ocean, for instance, chipmunks and mice share predators, and if the chipmunk population decreases, more mice will be eaten.

Competition between animals is an essential part of ecology. It determines species distribution, population dynamics, food webs, and social dominance hierarchies. These interactions result in a variety of physical and behavioral adaptations, which are a direct result of competition.

Competition among animals occurs naturally in nature, but human activities, invasive species, and other factors are constant stressors on ecosystems. The pressure from these factors affects their ability to co-exist.

DIRECT OR INDIRECT

An unregulated free market for organs would be a significant departure from the current system. Such a market would be unlikely to provide the benefits that its advocates promise.

Such policies would most likely involve limited financial incentives defined through administrative procedures and provided under highly regulated conditions. While examining the case for such a market may be helpful, it is unlikely to deliver the benefits that its advocates have promised. However, there are a few ways that a free market for organs might be better governed.

Organ players from around the world take part in the Canadian International Organ Competition. This international organ competition draws virtuosi under 35 from all over the world. The documentary, Pipe Dreams, follows four ultra-talented organ players as they prepare for the competition.

The film reveals the high mental discipline and dedication that go into competing for the top prize. While some organists are favored by the judges, others do not have the ability to compete on such a high level.

SURVIVAL OF THE FITTEST

The phrase "survival of the fittest" has many interpretations, and there are different ways of understanding how this term works. Essentially, survival of the fittest refers to the ability of organisms to survive and reproduce in a particular environment.

Organisms with the best survival rate will outcompete organisms with poorer survival rates, a concept which is fundamental to natural selection. Regardless of whether you are a plant, animal, or human, survival of the fittest is the key.

Despite its neo-Darwinian appeal, evolution has proven to be a challenging concept. In many ways, survival of the fittest is a theory of evolution, but it has yet to be proven.

New infections trigger natural selection and cause organisms to change. The recent coronavirus pandemic illustrates the challenge that the concept poses. A patient's immune response to the infection determines whether the patient survives.

It has been hypothesized that organ competitions may follow a similar process. In organ competition, neighbouring cells will sense the presence of an improved cell and compete to keep it.

But unlike organ competitions that are driven by competition among cells, it is not about getting rid of defective cells. The aim of cell competition is to preserve organ quality. Cells are competing for the same resources, so they are often stronger and more resilient than their neighbours.

EVOLUTION

In the evolution of life, organisms compete with one another for resources are scarce. In areas with abundant resources, organisms can coexist, but when they don't, competition can result in the elimination of one species from a shared environment.

This phenomenon occurs when an organism with a limited life history or a low competitive capacity faces competition from a more highly resource-efficient species. If a species has a low competitive capacity, it may be eliminated by competition, resulting in a decline in its population.

Intraspecific competition occurs between organisms within the same species. This type of competition improves the adaptability of each species. Interspecific competition occurs when organisms from different species compete for the same resources or share the same niche.

The more similar the organisms are, the more likely they are to exclude each other. If one species is more efficient than another, it may become extinct. Nonetheless, this type of competition may lead to both species becoming more specialized.

ECOLOGY

In Ecology, Organism Competition is an important part of the overall ecosystem. Competition among organisms occurs when resource supplies are scarce or overlap. For example, animals compete for food, water, and mineral resources, while plants compete for root space.

The result is competition, which leads to species diversity and the spread of diseases. Competition can be both beneficial and harmful, so understanding the process is important to understanding the way ecosystems work. Listed below are some of the ways in which Organism Competition can help us understand the world around us.

The main idea behind competition is that species of similar ecological niches cannot coexist. Competition results in the extinction of the less competitive species. This process is fundamental to the ecology of the natural world.

In other words, competition is inevitable. But the mechanisms by which competition occurs may be different for different species. Some species may compete with each other, while others may simply be rivals. The most common forms of competition are between intra and interspecific species.

Exploitative competition occurs between species. It is an important feature of many competitive interactions. In one study, a native thrip species became competitively dominant over an invasive species, requiring more time to feed and guard resources.

The latter species, in turn, decreased the amount of food available to itself and displaced its native counterpart. Other examples of both exploitative and interference competition are seen in plants. Some plants compete for space for root growth, while others suppress the growth of their competitors.

EVOLUTIONARY PROCESS

Competition is a natural selection mechanism that occurs between different organisms. It can increase the strength of selection and speed up adaptation. As competition increases, populations can adapt faster and can survive new environmental conditions better.

However, it can also have a negative impact on evolution. The effects of competition on evolution are dependent on the level of adaptation and the abundance of organisms relative to the critical abundance. The following paragraphs discuss the various effects of competition on organisms.

CPSIA information can be obtained
at www.ICGtesting.com
Printed in the USA
LVHW071912191222
735554LV00017B/723